Appointed to Wrath - Appointed to Salvation

Why Preach the Truth?

Moreno Dal Bello

APPOINTED TO WRATH - APPOINTED TO SALVATION

"For God hath not appointed us to Wrath, but to obtain salvation by our Lord Jesus Christ, Who died for us..." (1 Thessalonians 5:9,10).

For many people who consider themselves to be Christian the above Scriptures support the false teaching that no man is appointed to God's Wrath because Christ died for everyone. Others say that the Wrath spoken of here is in reference to the Wrath of Christ on the day of His return and not about the *eternal* Wrath of God. This latter teaching is immediately exposed as erroneous by pointing out that those appointed to Wrath are contrasted with those who will obtain eternal salvation. **Eternal because Christ's Sacrificial death is involved: *"...that He should give eternal life to as many as Thou hast given Him"*** (John 17:2). It is of matters eternal which are being spoken about here and not temporal. **Eternal salvation contrasted with eternal Wrath.** For the ignorant what corroborates their erroneous understanding of these Scriptures is the complete oversight as to exactly who the writer is referring to when he speaks of **"us"**. They have either totally overlooked the matter of, do not realise the import of this issue or have simply not been taught, who the writer has written his Letter to. Once you discover **who** the *us* is a reference to in verses 9 and 10 your understanding of **what** these Scriptures are saying, and what they could not possibly be saying, will be an accurate one and not a perverted one. **It is of the utmost importance that one realise just who the author of this Scripture is addressing and who he is not.** Paul is here **not** addressing every individual ever born but as an outcome of this study it will become increasingly self-evident that his words are exclusively directed to Christians.

Let us search the Scriptures. In verse 1 he begins his Epistle thusly: ***"Paul, and Silvanus and Timotheus, UNTO THE CHURCH of the Thessalonians"*** (1 Thessalonians 1:1). Clearly, unequivocally and without fear of contradiction, this opening to Paul's first Letter to the Thessalonians alone should leave no one in any doubt as to whom the author is addressing. **It is the Church, the called out ones of God.** Paul has not written to every individual living in Thessalonica but **only** to the Christians at Thessalonica. **No one else is intended and no one else could possibly be included in this**

group other than Christians. Of that there can be no Biblically based argument. Once this vital truth is established in the reader's mind they will be well under way to a proper understanding of just who is intended in the author's use of the word *us*, and which doctrines are being taught here. The false teaching that foolishly claims that by Paul's use of the word *us* he is referring to everyone the world over, the human race as a whole, can only lead one into doctrinal error and invariably into the murky depths of heretical doctrine. **This is all highly significant for false gospels and false teachers the world over have popularized error and in turn done much to gain wide acceptance for it is based on the misinformation poured forth concerning what God's Word actually says including the verses at hand.**

In the ensuing verses of the same chapter the apostle Paul goes on to make it even more abundantly clear to whom exactly he is writing: *"We give thanks to God always for you all, making mention of you in our prayers; Remembering without ceasing your work of faith, and labor of love, and patience of hope in our Lord Jesus Christ, in the sight of God and our Father; Knowing, brethren beloved, your election of God"* (1

Thessalonians 1:2-4). In light of these Scriptures I fail to see how even the most ardent and unrelenting of Arminians could dare venture to say that Paul is not here addressing his Letter exclusively to Christians, but to believer and unbeliever alike. Paul speaks of thanking God for the people he is writing to, that he remembers their work of faith, and labor of love, and patience of hope in the Lord Jesus. Paul clearly states that his Father and their Father is one and the same, referring to God as *"OUR Father"*. In the final verse of our passage, Paul refers to these ones he is addressing as **BRETHREN** and **BELOVED**. Clearly terms which are synonymous with, and exclusive to, Christians (see Romans 1:7; 9:25; 11:28; 1 Corinthians 15:58; Philippians 4:1; Colossians 3:12; 2 Thessalonians 2:13; James 1:19). These terms are **never** used in the whole of Scripture to describe non-Christians or Christian and non-Christian alike. Paul shows irrefutably here that he is writing to those who have been **ELECTED** of God, chosen by God to obtain salvation. He is writing to his fellow believers his **BRETHREN**. So it is established and confirmed, then, except to the blindest of the blind, that Paul is unquestionably addressing Christians in his first Letter to the Thessalonians and no one else.

So, then, what exactly does this undeniable fact have to do with our Scripture study from 1 Thessalonians 5:9 and 10? Why are we spending so much time on it? In light of what we have learned it is obvious to every reasonable person and in accordance to every grammatical law of the English language, and how it is used, that any use of the words *us*, *we* or *our* in Paul's Letter are undeniable references to Christians and Christians only. No other person or persons can rightly be inferred by the reader apart from the elect of God. And no Scripture supports such a grossly incorrect assertion as would claim that Paul's Letter is some kind of open letter to every individual ever born. All this has everything to do with having a proper and Biblically accurate understanding of just who this Letter has been written to and therefore what is being taught in 1 Thessalonians and what is not being taught at all. **Without establishing this fact, without knowing precisely whom Paul is writing to here, all one is left with is conjecture and speculation and, as a consequence, a never-ending argument as to what exactly verses 9 and 10 actually mean.** Once it is established to whom this Letter is addressed we may continue on with confidence knowing that we shall have a far greater ability to understand the doctrinal aspects of what Paul is saying in his Letter than those who will disregard what we have shown and simply deny the undeniable and refuse to believe he has addressed it solely to his fellow believers.

Chapter 5 of Paul's first Letter to the Thessalonians begins with Paul calling the Christians at Thessalonica, **"brethren"**. This, again, clearly shows that his Letter is not addressed to anyone and everyone at Thessalonica, let alone everyone in the entire world, but only to those Gospel believers who resided in Thessalonica. If I have written a letter to Bill and specifically addressed it to Bill, then only a fool, who neither knows Bill or I, would think that the letter was written to him or to both Bill and him. The apostle here calls those he writes to, 'brethren'. It must be pointed out that the word 'brethren' here qualifies every Gospel believer who would come to read this Letter, indeed the New Testament, to believe that this includes them also (see John 17:20). Further on, in verses 4 and 5, Paul says this: **"But ye, brethren, are not in darkness, that that day should overtake you as a thief. Ye are all the children of Light, and the children of the Day: we are not of the night, nor of darkness"** (1 Thessalonians 5:4,5). Paul has been speaking concerning the day of the Lord's return and again addresses those to whom he writes as *"**brethren**"*. He calls them all the **children of Light** and **children of the Day**. Then, and this will leave no doubt in anyone's mind except for those who simply will not see, Paul includes *himself* along with those he is writing to, saying ***"WE are not of the night, nor of darkness"***. Therefore it is safe, right and proper to conclude that Paul is indeed writing to Christians. They are brethren of Paul's and he of them. They are of the Day not of the night and are not in darkness for they, along with Paul and Silvanus and Timotheus are indeed the children of Light.

With this truth firmly established and supported by numerous Scriptures we go on and turn our attention to the main Scriptures pertaining to our study: ***"For God hath not appointed us to wrath, but to obtain salvation by our Lord Jesus Christ, Who died for us..."*** (1 Thessalonians 5:9,10). The word *us* here is a clear reference to those Paul is writing and includes himself as well as Silvanus and Timotheus and all the brethren who would follow in their steps. These ones who have been appointed by God to obtain salvation, are said, in verse 9, **NOT** to have been appointed by God to receive His Wrath. Paul clearly states that God HAS instead appointed them all to obtain salvation by their Lord Jesus Christ **WHO DIED FOR THEM. Now, if ever there was a passage of Scripture which contains such convincing proof as the ones I place before you which provide overwhelming evidence to support the teaching of election and that Christ's Sacrificial death was not for every individual ever born but exclusively for His people, those whom God gave to Him, those who have not been appointed to Wrath, as others, but who have been appointed to obtain salvation, it is these Scriptures.** These Scriptures are on a par with Romans 9 as being among the key Scriptures in the Word of God which clearly teach and defend the doctrines of salvation being by an election of grace, that the death of Christ was exclusively for the chosen of God. (for more on the doctrine of election please see my book 'Election is Just Not Fair!' at godsonlygospel.com)

Let us take a closer look now, at the first half of verse 9. Paul says, ***"God hath not appointed us to Wrath"***. Clearly, Paul is speaking of a people who have not been appointed to the Wrath of God. **The established fact that Paul is writing to believers, coupled with his use of the word 'us', is proof positive that he is referring to Christians here, those for**

whom Christ died, as not being among those appointed to Wrath. There is nothing else to conclude from these words but that God has not appointed, He has not made an appointment for, the apostle Paul or the people he is writing to, to receive His Wrath. In saying this we notice that the verse strongly implies that God HAS appointed some to Wrath but not these people, the believers, who have alternatively been appointed to obtain salvation. **Only some will receive God's Wrath and therefore only some will obtain salvation.** Obviously then those who will receive God's Wrath are those whom He has not appointed to obtain salvation but rather who have been specifically and purposely appointed to receive His Wrath. **So then it is right and proper to conclude that not all will suffer the Wrath of God and not all will obtain salvation.** Those who have been appointed to God's Wrath **will not** obtain salvation, and those who have been appointed to obtain salvation **will not** receive God's Wrath. **The Scripture teaches that it is God who elects those whom He will save and those who will receive His Wrath**(see Romans 9:8,11,13,15,16,18,21,22). So then, if it is not all who will receive the Wrath of God, if it is not all who have been appointed to His Wrath, then it must be that not all will obtain salvation by His

Son. **To properly, Scripturally, accept one of these teachings is to accept the other also.** If not all have been appointed to obtain salvation by the Lord Jesus Christ then it is a given that some have been appointed to Wrath, **but clearly not** those who have been appointed to obtain salvation which is precisely what these Scriptures are saying.

Now notice what makes the difference between the two groups. Why are some appointed to Wrath and some to obtain salvation? **Not only is it a matter of God's appointing but it has everything to do with who Christ died for.** The second half of our Scripture study says: *"...but to obtain salvation by our Lord Jesus Christ, Who died for us..."*(1 Thessalonians 5:9,10). What this second half of the Scriptures from 1 Thessalonians 5:9,10 is saying is: *'God has appointed us* (believers) *to obtain salvation through Jesus Christ Who died for us'*. **Notice that this salvation does not come simply by appointment alone, but through the means of Christ's death exclusively for those who have not been appointed to Wrath but who have been appointed to obtain salvation.** Evidently, there are two groups of people involved here: those who have been appointed to God's Wrath and not salvation, and those who have been appointed by God to obtain salvation and not Wrath. **Those for whom Christ did not die and those for whom Christ did die. These Scriptures teach, and are forever linked to, the inescapable fact that Jesus Christ the Lord did not die for everyone.**

Christ the Savior did not die for those whom the Father has appointed to His Wrath. Christ, however, did die, He offered Himself to the Father as a Substitutionary Sacrifice, only for those whom He HAS appointed to obtain salvation and NOT those whom the Father has appointed to Wrath. YOU SIMPLY CANNOT BREAK THE CHAIN WHICH GOD HAS LINKED BETWEEN THE APPOINTMENT OF SOME TO OBTAIN SALVATION AND CHRIST'S DEATH. This appointment to salvation is eternally connected, and only achievable by the Lord Jesus Christ Who died exclusively for those whom the Father has appointed to obtain salvation. (For a detailed study of the Atonement of Christ and what His Sacrificial death means please see my book 'Atonement for Whom?: A Study of the High Priesthood of Christ' at godsonlygospel.com).

According to the apostle Paul, the *brethren*, the *beloved*, *the children of Light*, *the children of the Day*, the very *elect of God*, the *chosen of*

God will **NOT** be among the recipients of the Wrath of God for they have not been appointed thereunto but to salvation by the Lord Jesus Christ **WHO DIED FOR THEM! THAT IS THE DIFFERENCE MAKER!** Two Scriptures which will further cement this great truth may be found in the Letter to the Hebrews. *"Wherefore He is able also to save them to the uttermost that come unto God by Him* (Jesus)*, seeing He ever liveth to make intercession FOR THEM"* (Hebrews 7:25). The Lord Jesus Himself tells us who exactly they are for whom He prays: *"I have manifested Thy name unto the men which Thou gavest me out of the world....I pray for them: I pray not for the world, but for them which Thou hast given Me; for they are Thine....Neither pray I for these alone, but for them also which shall believe on Me through their word"* (John 17:6,9,20). We see here how CHRIST HIMSELF DECLARES that He prays only for those whom God has given Him. **Jesus Christ does not pray for those whom the Father has not given Him. Christ prays only for God's people.** Link all of these verses with the following and it paints a clear and distinct picture of whom it is for whom Christ died: *"And for this cause He is the Mediator of the New Testament, that*

BY MEANS OF DEATH, for the redemption of the transgressions that were under the first Testament, THEY WHICH ARE CALLED might receive the promise of eternal inheritance" (Hebrews 9:15). YES, it is true! There is an elect of God and Christ Jesus DID die, He laid down His life for HIS people, the elect of God, **the God-appointed ones**, the ones whom God had chosen before the very foundation of the world and given, entrusted, to His Son Jesus Christ (see John 17:2 & Ephesians 1:4), to make sacrifice for because not a single one of them was appointed to Wrath but rather they were all appointed to obtain salvation **by Him**. THIS is the word of God: **"...GOD HATH NOT APPOINTED US TO WRATH, BUT TO OBTAIN SALVATION BY OUR LORD JESUS CHRIST, WHO DIED FOR US"** (1 Thessalonians 5:9). What a statement! What a declaration! What an irrefutable truth!

It is no minor detail that God's appointing works both ways: The Sovereign God appoints some to Wrath and some to Salvation. Significantly, **Scripture does not teach** that God appoints some to salvation and leaves the others to themselves. NO. He appoints one group just as much as He appoints the other. **Therefore, you cannot rightly believe God appoints one**

group without believing that He also appoints the other group. Romans 9 spells this out clearly: *"Hath not the potter power over the clay, of the same lump to make one vessel unto honor, and another unto dishonor?"* (Romans 9:21). Notice God has **made** TWO things here. He has, of the same lump, **made** one vessel unto honor, and He has, of the same lump, **made** another vessel unto dishonor. **Two items were made and not merely one and the rest of the clay left formless.** Significantly, Paul goes on to talk about *"..vessels of Wrath fitted to destruction..."* and later *"...vessels of mercy, which He had afore prepared unto glory, Even US, whom He hath called..."* (Romans 9:22-24). God is the Potter and not only is the clay His but He made the clay. God has made one vessel unto honor and He has made one vessel unto dishonor. **Those He has made vessels unto dishonor are those vessels of Wrath fitted to destruction, those appointed unto His Wrath.** Proverbs 16:4 tells us: *"The Lord hath made all things for Himself: yea, even the wicked for the day of evil"*. Those who are made vessels unto honor are called vessels of mercy which God had before prepared, not to receive His Wrath, but these are the ones He has prepared unto glory, the ones HE HAS CALLED. **How could the Lord have made His Scriptures any clearer?**

The only reason there is disagreement and argument and controversy to do with the Scriptures is because of those people who are blind to them and think they are saved but are lost. Who think they are Christian but are not. Who think they have the truth of God but they do not. ***"If any man teach otherwise, and consent not to wholesome words, even the words of our Lord Jesus Christ, and to the doctrine which is according to Godliness; he is proud, knowing nothing, but doting about questions and strifes of words, whereof cometh envy, strife, railings, evil surmisings, Perverse disputings of men of corrupt minds, and destitute of the truth, supposing that gain is godliness: from such withdraw thyself"*** (1 Timothy 6:3-5 cf. Isaiah 8:20). The divisions and controversies do not come from those who teach right doctrine but from those who teach contrary to right doctrine: ***"Now I beseech you, brethren, mark them which cause divisions and offences contrary to the doctrine which ye have learned; and avoid them. For they that are such serve not our Lord Jesus Christ, but their own belly; and by***

good words and fair speeches deceive the hearts of the simple" (Romans 16:17,18 cf. Galatians 1:8,9).

There are two groups, and there have always been two groups of people, who walk this earth: **those whom God has appointed to His Wrath and those whom He has appointed to obtain Salvation.** Those who are the goats and those who are the sheep (see Matthew 25). Those who are the called out ones who make up His Church, the Body of Christ, and those who are not the called out ones. **Those for whom Christ died and those for whom He did not die.** Those who have been appointed to obtain salvation and those who have, not merely not been appointed to obtain salvation, but who have been appointed to Wrath. Spiritual blindness, which can at best only ever provide a perverted view of the Scriptures, has never been more evident than in the preposterousness of the lies that in light of these Scriptures: **a)** God has, purely by His grace, not appointed any to salvation for one must choose Him; **b)** that God is a God of love Who would never appoint any to receive His wrath; **c)** that God has appointed some for whom Christ died to also receive His Wrath; **d)** that God has appointed everyone to obtain salvation, and therefore **e)** that Christ died for everyone. **The truth of the matter is: God has purely by His grace appointed some to obtain salvation by the death of His Glorious Son Jesus Christ; God has appointed all those for whom Christ did not die to receive His Wrath; Christ's Atoning death was exclusively for the sheep, the Church, the ones entrusted to Him by the Father; the ones whom the Father has appointed to obtain salvation:** *"I am the Good Shepherd: the Good Shepherd giveth His life for THE SHEEP"* (John 10:11 cf. 10:15); *"Husbands, love your wives, even as Christ also loved the Church, and gave Himself for IT"* (Ephesians 5:25); Whom did Christ die for? **THE ONES HE LOVED!** The ones appointed to obtain salvation through His death. *"And Thou hast given Him power over all flesh, that He should give eternal life TO AS MANY AS THOU HAST GIVEN HIM"* (John 17:2); *"For God hath not appointed US to Wrath, but to obtain Salvation by our Lord Jesus Christ, Who died for US..."* (1 Thessalonians 5:9,10). Christ loved the Church not the world, for He did not even pray for the world *"I pray for them: I pray not for the world, but for them which Thou hast given me; for they are Thine...."I have chosen you out of the world..."* (John 17:9;

15:19). Here we see Christ's exclusive love for the Church, those for whom He prays whom God has given to Him. So Christ prays only for His people revealed here as the ones God has given Him, and in John 17:2 it is revealed that only these ones are to be the recipients of eternal life, the only ones for whom Christ would die. **And yet millions believe Christ died for everyone!** Christ loves the sheep for whom He laid down His life and not the goats (see John 10:15). And Christ's Sacrificial death was for all those whom the Father gave unto Him, the Church, all those who have been appointed to obtain salvation through Christ Who died for **them. How could Christ have died for anyone who was not first given unto Him by the Father, who was not first appointed to obtain salvation through Christ's death? How could Christ have died for anyone for whom He did not pray, for those who were not given unto Him by the Father but who have been appointed to God's Wrath? No one for whom Christ died will perish and not one for whom Christ did not die will receive eternal life**

In appointing some to obtain salvation through the death of Christ, it is clear from Scripture that Christ Jesus the Lord died for those people and not for any others. **For anyone**

outside of that group of appointees have, in contrast, been appointed to the Wrath of God. What purpose would there have been for Jesus Christ to offer His Substitutionary Sacrifice for the vessels fitted to destruction, when clearly such people have not been appointed to obtain salvation, which is the fruit of Christ's death, but are appointed to Wrath? **Such people were not appointed to obtain salvation because Christ did not die for them and vice versa!** In light of this, saying Christ died for everyone is tantamount to saying that those people appointed to Wrath, the ones not appointed to obtain salvation, would obtain salvation anyway! That, in some mystical way, those appointed to Wrath have also been appointed to salvation! Sheer lunacy. The fact that Christ died for those appointed to obtain salvation links up perfectly with the words of Jesus Himself in John 17 where He says to the Father: *"As Thou hast given Him power over all flesh, that He should give eternal life to as many as Thou hast given Him"* (John 17:2). **How could these people given to Christ be any other people apart from the ones God has chosen before the foundation of the world to be His people?** Only those given to Christ are those for whom He prayed and died. **Only those given to**

Christ are the ones that have been appointed to obtain salvation. Eternal life which is in Jesus Christ is given, not to as many as would choose Him as the Arminian would have you believe, but to as many as the Father has *given*, *granted*, *supplied*, *committed to*, *entrusted*, or appointed, to His Son.

Salvation is God's business, He has elected who will be saved and who will not, and those He has given to His Son can be none other than those whom He has chosen before the foundation of the world that salvation might be by grace and not by works: *"According as HE HATH CHOSEN US in Him before the foundation of the world...HAVING PREDESTINATED US...according to the good pleasure of HIS WILL, to the praise of the glory of His GRACE, wherein HE HATH MADE US ACCEPTED in the Beloved"* (Ephesians 1:4-6; see also Philippians 1:29). Interestingly, the word here *predestinated* means *to predetermine, decide beforehand, God decreeing from eternity, to foreordain, APPOINT beforehand*. **God has predestinated US to obtain salvation through the death of the Lord Jesus Christ.**

In the apostle Peter's first Letter he, too, is addressing only Christians. Peter wrote to *"...the strangers scattered throughout Pontus, Galatia, Cappadocia, Asia and Bithynia, ELECT according to the foreknowledge of God the Father"* (1 Peter 1:1,2). Like Paul, Peter goes on in the same chapter to group himself with those he is writing to, in verse 3: *"Blessed be The God and Father of OUR Lord Jesus Christ, which according to His abundant mercy hath begotten US again unto a lively hope by the Resurrection of Jesus Christ from the dead"* (1 Peter 1:3). Further on in his second chapter Peter describes these people as: *"...a chosen generation, a royal priesthood, an holy nation, a peculiar people; that ye should show forth the praises of Him Who hath called you out of darkness into His marvelous Light"* (1 Peter 2:9). Again we see a group of people, **beloved of God, the brethren**, who have been chosen of God who are not in darkness but who have been called into His marvelous Light. **Children of Light** just as Paul called the brethren he wrote to at Thessalonica. Interestingly, the preceding two verses contain very familiar language as used in Paul's first Letter to the Thessalonians. Peter writes: *"Unto you therefore which believe He is precious: but unto them which be disobedient, the stone which the builders disallowed, the same is*

made the head of the corner, and a stone of stumbling, and a rock of offence, even to them which stumble at the word, being disobedient: WHEREUNTO ALSO THEY WERE APPOINTED" (1 Peter 2:7,8). Notably, the word *appointed* here is the same one used by Paul in 1 Thessalonians 5:9. In 1 Peter 2 we see that these ones whom Peter referred to as *a chosen generation*, in contrast with those he referred to as appointed to disobedience, as the people of God: ***"Which in time past were not a people, but are now the people of God..."*** (1 Peter 2:10). Only those who are **not** the people of God, who have rejected the true Christ, are said to be disobedient **and it is to this disobedience they were appointed**. Now, do you think that any for whom Christ died are among these? Like Paul, Peter here clearly defines two groups: the one which is disobedient, rejecters of Christ, and the other to whom Christ is precious. To say that Christ died for the disobedient, those who would reject Him, as well as those who count Him precious is to say that Christ's death achieved salvation for some but not for others. It is to say that Christ died both for those who have been appointed to Wrath as well as those appointed to obtain salvation. **In light of the Scriptures presented in this article, that Christ did not**

die for those appointed to Wrath but only for those appointed to obtain salvation, is the only teaching that makes any Biblical sense here. To say Christ died for everyone is to say that salvation is not based on grace, **something which God does**, making the difference between saved and lost. To say that God did not arbitrarily elect those whom He would save is to have a 'salvation' that cannot be founded upon Christ's Righteousness alone, but by a man's free will choice, **something that he does. Such a blasphemous concept as this runs counter to our Scriptures which place a distinct difference between those whom God has appointed to receive His Wrath and those whom He has appointed to Salvation through Christ's dying for them.** CHRIST'S DEATH IS FOREVER LINKED EXCLUSIVELY TO THOSE WHOM THE FATHER HAS APPOINTED TO OBTAIN SALVATION

Do you think that the people for whom Christ died, who were not appointed to God's Wrath but to obtain salvation and eternal life through Him, would ever end up being disobedient, i.e. rejecting the Savior? **The fact that God elected them before the foundation of the world and that Christ died for them shows that they were all appointed, NOT to**

reject Him, NOT to disobey Him, but to receive Him, and love Him and obtain salvation through Him! They were not given temporary life but ETERNAL LIFE in Him. THESE ARE VESSELS OF MERCY WHICH GOD HAS PREPARED UNTO **GLORY** NOT DESTRUCTION! **These are the ONLY ones God loves, evidenced by the Father giving ONLY them to His Son, choosing ONLY them before the foundation of the world to be His children and appointing ONLY these select ones, these loved ones for whom Christ would die, to salvation.** If Christ has died for you then you believe/will believe His glorious Gospel of grace as His only power unto salvation and no other and so you are not appointed to Wrath but to obtain Salvation through the Messiah's death, through His Sacrifice for you, in place of you, on your behalf, for your salvation. *"Neither by the blood of goats and calves, but by His own blood He entered in once into the Holy Place, having obtained eternal redemption for US"* (Hebrews 9:12). You see Christ's death was not a scatter shot into the crowd in hope that some would be affected. Christ's death was for a specific group of people, it was specifically aimed, with sniper like accuracy if you will, at God's chosen, those whom He had appointed to obtain salvation through Christ's death, His Sacrifice, for those people He has obtained eternal redemption for. Christ's death was not something made and offered to every individual ever born, its effectiveness made operational upon each individual's acceptance of it, for Christ's Sacrifice was offered to, and accepted by, the Father. Speaking to the saints, believers, at Ephesus, Paul states: *"...walk in love, as Christ hath also loved US, and hath given Himself FOR US an offering and a sacrifice TO GOD for a sweetsmelling savour"* (Ephesians 5:2).

Moreover, do you think that for one minute God has appointed those for whom His Son died to obtain salvation AND to receive His Wrath? But how can they be appointed to receive Wrath when Christ Jesus the Savior, **by His death for them** has blotted out their sins that were against them nailing them to His cross? *"And you, being dead in your sins and the uncircumcision of your flesh, hath He quickened together with Him, having forgiven you ALL trespasses; Blotting out the handwriting of ordinances that was against us, which was contrary to us, and took it out of the way, nailing it to His cross"* (Colossians 2:13,14). **Everyone who will receive the Wrath of God has been appointed thereunto and so could not** possibly be among those for whom Christ died. Likewise, everyone who has/will obtain salvation has been appointed thereunto by the Holy God and will never receive of His Wrath.

Are you of the belief that any who have been appointed to Wrath are among those for whom Christ died? Do you honestly believe that anyone for whom Christ died will not obtain salvation but instead receive the Wrath of God, something which Scripture says they are NOT appointed to receive? How could this be when clearly 1 Thessalonians 5 is speaking of two distinct groups. THERE IS NO ROOM IN EITHER GROUP FOR ANY MORE APPOINTEES! NO DUAL APPOINTMENTS HAVE BEEN MADE! NO ONE HAS BEEN DOUBLE BOOKED! **Those who have been appointed to God's Wrath have not been appointed to salvation and are therefore those for whom Christ did not die. If Christ did die for them what would they be doing among those who have been appointed unto Wrath? And, those who have been appointed to obtain salvation, through Jesus Christ, have not been appointed to God's Wrath and are therefore those for whom Christ did die.** It is all so simple isn't it when one is given the Gift of

Faith which comes from God to rightly understand what the Scriptures are really saying and not what the blind, the lost, perceive them to be saying.

And so, we beg the question again, do you believe for one minute that God who has appointed some to Wrath would include among them His very own people? Do you for one minute believe that God has appointed some to obtain salvation through the death of Christ, whom He calls his very own people, would include even one of these people to also obtain His Wrath? It is absurd to say the least. There is nothing in Scripture that has ever supported such fables as these. It is only the blinded minds of the lost that have embraced such lies and I am afraid their lustful affair continues.

To those who are saved, who have been given the Gift of Faith to see, understand and believe the doctrines of the Gospel of the Grace of God, salvation is purely and wholly by grace. It is solely a Work of God and not something which is achieved by God and man. The Bible says God chooses some and not others. God has chosen a people for Himself out of the world. These ones are they whom God has appointed to obtain salvation through the death of His dear Son the Lord Jesus. The

rest have been appointed to God's eternal Wrath. They are not the children of light for they reside in darkness. They are the children of the night who shall never see the Day. The children of the Day, however, will never experience the Wrath of God for they, by His Great Grace, have been appointed to obtain Salvation.

REPENT AND BELIEVE HIS GOSPEL

WHY PREACH THE TRUTH?

The whole purpose of teaching is to instruct people in the right way and to distinguish the right way from the wrong ways, proving why the truth is the truth and why anything which contradicts it, is not. To teach is to declare the truth and prove why it is the truth thus leading the people away from an erroneous understanding of it, and so exposing error. The right way has its consequences and the wrong way has its consequences. **And when it comes to the Gospel of God, right teaching and wrong teaching is a matter of what God has said and what God has not said -- The Truth of God and the lies of men -- "*...the Spirit of Truth, and the spirit of error*"** (1 Jn. 4:6). **What God has said is right and what God has not said is wrong.** If you believe what God has said, you are right. You have the Truth. If you do not believe what God has said, but only what is claimed God has said, you are wrong because you believe in that which is not God's Truth. You are an unbeliever and Scripture declares you a liar and a false witness of the true God rather than a believer in Him (see 1 Jn. 5:10 & 1 Cor. 15:14,15). **Salvation is all about knowing God, believing in the true God and not in a false god which cannot save.** To believe in the true God is to believe in the doctrines of the Gospel of the grace of God in the salvation of His people.**Without the true knowledge of God there can be no salvation.** The true knowledge of Who God is, what God has done and for whom He has done it. **The knowledge of the Gospel of God.** To know and believe the true God is to know and believe the true Gospel of God which is to know and believe the true doctrines of that Gospel which reveal, define and distinguish the true God and His true Christ from all impostors. The Gospel of God is revealed to all God's people. **All God's chosen are given eyes to see and ears to hear. By Grace they are granted the gift of Faith by God to believe His Gospel and reject all others.** That is, to believe the truth about God and how He saves, and to reject the lies about Him contained in gospels which are not of God. **The Gospel of Christ is God's Instrument by which He delivers the doctrines of Truth about Christ which is essential to a saving knowledge of Him.**"*According as His Divine power hath given unto us all things that pertain unto life and godliness, <u>through the knowledge of Him</u> that hath called us to glory and virtue*" (2 Pet. 1:3). **Without the knowledge of the doctrines of the Gospel of God's Grace there can be no salvation.** The apostle Paul states *"But if our Gospel be hid* (veiled, not known), *it is hid to them that are lost"* (2 Cor. 4:3). Without the knowledge of the Gospel of God and the Faith with which to savingly believe it, there can be no salvation. *"...Faith cometh by hearing, and hearing by the Word of*

God" (Rom. 10:17). **Faith does not, indeed cannot, come without the hearing of the Word of God's Gospel. The Gospel of God must be preached to every creature for salvation cannot take place before, or without, the hearing and believing of the Gospel of God.** The apostle Paul writing to the Christians at Ephesus noted that their trusting in Christ occurred ***"...after that ye heard the Word of Truth, the Gospel of your salvation: in Whom also after ye believed, ye were sealed with that Holy Spirit of promise"*** (Eph. 1:13).

Christ commanded ***"...repent ye, and believe the Gospel"*** (Mk. 1:15). Faith and repentance are inseparable. The gift of repentance from God always brings with it the acknowledgment of the truth of God and does not leave anyone in a perpetual state of rejection of it or ignorance concerning it. ***"...if God peradventure will give them repentance to the acknowledging of the truth"*** (2 Timothy 2:25). A repentance which does not acknowledge the truth of God, is not the gift of repentance which God gives to all His people. **No acknowledgement of God's Gospel = no true repentance = no salvation.** One cannot properly acknowledge the truth without rejecting error. If a person claims to believe God's true Gospel and yet still clings to any false gospel, or to even one of its false doctrines, they previously believed rather than rejecting it as having any power to save, then they cannot be a true believer in God's Gospel as being His ONLY power unto salvation (see Rom. 1:16). **"Paul, a servant of God, and an apostle of Jesus Christ, according to THE <u>Faith</u> of God's elect, and the <u>acknowledging of the truth</u> which is after godliness"** (Titus 1:1). Notice that there is only one Faith which is common to the elect of God (see also Jude 3), and only with that gift of Faith can one savingly acknowledge the truth of God **"Who will have all men to be saved, and to come unto the<u>knowledge of the truth</u>"** (1 Timothy 2:4 cf. Romans 10:2; Philippians 3:8). **Again, the connection between salvation and knowledge.** Importantly, knowledge does not gain us salvation. **Knowledge does not save anyone but it is the evidence, or fruit, of salvation.** Anyone can claim to know and believe in the true answer to a mathematical equation but only those who do know it, and can actually tell you what the true answer is, provide the evidence necessary to be judged correct. **There is no salvation without the knowledge of the Truth of God.** Knowledge does not save anyone but no one is saved without it. To be saved is to pass from spiritual darkness to the Light of the glorious Gospel of Christ, the knowledge of His Truth (see 2 Corinthians 4:3,4). Look carefully at Titus 1:1-3 and notice the distinct connection between **the <u>FAITH</u> of God's elect; the <u>ACKNOWLEDGING</u> of the <u>TRUTH</u>; <u>GODLINESS</u>; in hope of <u>ETERNAL LIFE</u>; and manifestedHis <u>WORD</u> through <u>PREACHING</u>.**

The Faith which is given to everyone of God's elect is given so that they will all acknowledge the Truth of God, rather than speculate as to what it could be as those of the world do who know not God. **To be a true Christian is to KNOW!** In Romans 10, Paul asks how can any call on the true God if they do not believe on Him; and how can any rightly believe on Him if they have not heard of Him: *"...and how shall they hear without a preacher?"* (Rom. 10:14). And what is it which they must hear? Paul continues *"...How beautiful are the feet of them that preach the Gospel of peace..."* (Rom. 10:15).

Now, if salvation does not hinge upon belief of God's Gospel of peace then the truth simply would not matter at all, and therefore needs not be preached. If actually believing what God has said concerning salvation does not matter, then truth is relative, indeed, what God says about salvation, His Son, the Gospel becomes merely a relative thing. Therefore the truth would be judged right or wrong as each individual saw fit. Truth would be judged according to how a person thinks. The truth of God would not need to be preached and believed for a man to be saved for he could just believe what he wants to believe and still be saved. Believing God's Truth and believing a man's lies, would all amount to the same thing. **If all this were true, the truth of what God has done, of how He saves, indeed, of Who God is, would not be important enough to figure in the salvation**

of anyone, for what a man believes the truth to be would have equal footing with what God says the truth is. The fact of the matter is that if God has said something, the onus is on man to believe it because you can be guaranteed that what God speaks is Truth, the whole Truth and nothing but the Truth, for God is Truth (see Jn. 14:6). Not believing what God has said will have dire and eternal consequences: ***"...in them that perish; because they received not the love of the Truth, that they might be saved....That they all might be damned who believed not the Truth..."*** (2 Thess. 2:10,12). Couple these two Scriptures with the following words of Christ Jesus Himself and you begin to see a clear picture of the essentiality of hearing, knowing and believing the Truth of God. The Lord's command to His people is to preach the Gospel to every creature: ***"He that believeth and is baptized shall be saved; but he that believeth not shall be damned"*** (Mk. 16:16).

No one has ever profited by not believing the Word of God, so how can any say that to not believe the Gospel, but to believe error concerning it, i.e. another gospel, will still save a person. This line of argument goes far beyond the boundaries of Scriptural reasoning. I mean, why preach the truth at all! Why warn of false preachers who come with false doctrines (see Matt. 24:24; 1 Jn. 4:1) if one can be just as saved by believing the lies they teach as one is in believing what true men of God, who preach His Gospel, say? **The**

main reason why teaching is necessary at all is the fact that the Word of God is the very instrument through which God expresses His Truth concerning His Son in the salvation of His people. This Truth is encapsulated in the Gospel of God. The Gospel of God reveals the true and only God. It shows Who He is, what He has done and for whom He has done it. The Gospel of God at once shows what was necessary to the salvation of God's people and exactly what and Who a saved man trusts. **The Gospel of God is the Truth of God and everything outside of that Gospel forms part of a gospel which the God of Truth has simply not authored. Any gospel which contradicts any doctrine of the true Gospel does not represent or present the true God.**

      Another reason why preaching and teaching the Gospel of God is necessary is because there is right and wrong, and the purpose behind proving that which is right as right is so a person will acknowledge and enjoy the Truth of God and reject the lies about God which present themselves as truth. So that a person will enjoy the benefits of being blessed of God to believe the truth, as opposed to believing error and remaining in an accursed state for all eternity. **But if whether one believes truth or error does not matter, that it is not the prime evidence of salvation, then there is no reason why anyone should teach anything, for believing whatever one believes to be the truth, as opposed to what the Truth of God actually is,**

would be one and the same thing! Therefore, a man can be saved regardless of whether he believes God's Testimony of His Son, or another's testimony of Him or simply your own idea, or version, of Him! *"Thus, in common with a fundamental tenet of the New Gnosticism—that there is no objective reality"*—the Gospel can be anything a person wants it to be and thus Who God is and how God saves would go from being Scriptural fact to something which would be open to interpretation. Let us all live in and for existential experiences and form our own doctrines and believe what we want to believe, is the rebellious cry of the 21st century. **Thus we see the aim of Satan: to create a worldwide religious climate where there are virtually no rules, no Standard of belief, where the lines between right and wrong, truth and falsehood, between true Gospel doctrine and the lies of false gospels, become so blurred as to make them indivisible. Where a man's views rather than God's Truth reign in the hearts of all men.**

When Christ Jesus the Lord commanded His people to *"...preach the Gospel to every creature"* (Mk. 16:15), He made no mention that preaching the Gospel of God meant what anyone thought the Gospel to be. Not even the slightest hint was given that the Gospel of God was of any private interpretation or to even the possibility of there being more than one Gospel. Christ made reference only to **THE GOSPEL**, God's Gospel, the one and only Gospel by which God saves. **God's**

Gospel reveals what a person must believe to show they are saved, that they have eternal life. Only belief in the Gospel of God is the sure sign of salvation "...*for it* **(the Gospel) *is the power of God unto salvation...*"** (Rom. 1:16). Christ also had a very clear message to those who will not believe HIS Gospel: ***"...he that believeth not shall be damned"*** (Mk. 16:16). This Scripture ties in perfectly with the apostle Paul's inspired declaration that ***"...if our Gospel be hid, it is hid to them that are LOST"*** (2 Cor. 4:3; 1 Jn. 5:10-13).

Therefore, we see clearly that the Truth, God's Holy Gospel Message concerning His grace in the salvation of His people through the Righteousness of His Son, must be preached by His people to every creature. **The Truth must be heard to be known and believed** (see Rom. 10:10-17). If truth matters at all then the Gospel of God matters. If believing simple truths like the correct answer to 2 +2 is 4 matters, then it surely must matter what the true Gospel of God is. **It matters what God's answers are to the questions, 'Who is Jesus?' 'What did He do' and 'For whom did He do it', as well as 'What must I do to be saved?' There is no salvation present in one's life if that life is free of the knowledge and Faith of God's Gospel by which God saves.** As in the world of Mathematics where no one is right if they do not have the correct answer, so too, in God's reality no one is saved unless they are believers in God's only power to save: **His Gospel**. This is not about intelligence, doctrinal regeneration or salvation by knowledge, but of **REVELATION! Believing God's Gospel and rejecting, repenting of, all others is the evidence that God has revealed His Gospel by His Holy Spirit to the heart and mind of a man.**

"...Faith cometh by hearing, and hearing by the Word of God" (Rom. 10:17).

REPENT AND BELIEVE THE GOSPEL OR YOU WILL DIE IN YOUR SINS

Please Contact:

morenodalbello@yahoo.com.au

Please Visit:

www.godsonlygospel.com

Made in the USA
Monee, IL
03 May 2026